— This insomniac land of Paris at night, it's the sea upon which the Night passes. This film. This ship adrift that they've named: Night.

In the day, nothing is seen of this passage of night.

In the day, nothing.

The movements of the ship named Night should testify to other movements happening elsewhere and of a different nature.

The movements of the ship named Night should testify to the movements of desire.

Marguerite Duras

SIX FILMS Le navire Night — Césarée — Les mains négatives —Aurélia Steiner — Aurélia Steiner — Aurélia Steiner

Translated by
Olivia Baes & Emma Ramadan

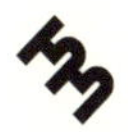

Mercurial Editions
New York City
MMXXV

The story in *The Ship Named Night* was told to me in December '77 by the person who had lived it, J. M., the young man of Les Gobelins. I knew J. M. and I knew the story. There were about ten of us who knew of its existence. But we had never spoken about it together, J. M. and I. It was after three years that one day—I had spoken about it with a friend of J. M. who said she had already forgotten certain details—I was afraid that the story would be lost. I asked J. M. to record it on tape. He agreed.

Apart from certain dates and the knot of names in Père Lachaise that he had never managed to disentangle, he remembered. Everything was still there. It was three years after the end of the story, F.'s wedding.

Hearing him tell it, I understood that J. M. had no doubt always hoped to bring this story face to face with a listener, but that he had always feared—when the moment came—that people wouldn't believe him "if he said everything."

And that rather than being troubled by it, he was happy to speak about it.

It was based on that tape recording that I wrote *The Ship Named Night*—twice over, with six months in between. The first version of the text is from February '78, it appeared in *Minuit* journal. The second version of the text is what is published here, it is the final text from the film shoot, July '78.

I gave the first version of the text to J. M. He read it. He said that "everything was true but that he recognized nothing." I asked him if I could publish it and then perhaps, later on, turn it into a film. He told me that he hoped I would. That day we stopped talking about the story. To tell the truth, never again. After having read what his own experience became—in the words of another—J. M. remained silent but as if he were always on the verge of speaking. I think he must have realized that other versions of his story were possible—that he had silenced them because he didn't know that they were possible just as they were possible for any story. I think too that his own version had carried him so far that he had forgotten its sprawl, its banality.

A few days after he read the text, J. M. called me, he told me that he had been consumed again by a desire for F. that was so strong—after reading the written story—that he wanted to know whether she was still alive and he asked me to use her full name—rather than her initials—in *Minuit*. So that F. would understand that he was calling out to her. I said that the initials seemed sufficient to me given that F. knew her name. He agreed.

Later, during the week that followed the film's release, I called J. M. He told me that he had received phone calls with no one at the other end of the line except for that presence, breathing, undeniable, which he knew was hers. Because that was already her behavior as their story was unfolding, to make sure he knew that she loved him still and so intensely that she might die from it.

The dying F. was still alive at the beginning of 1979. I haven't seen J. M. again since then.

I didn't distribute the text of *The Ship Named Night* among those who spoke it in the film. There were only dashes before the sentences to indicate that the speaker should change at this or that moment of the narrative. Similarly, I didn't specify the order of the shots or describe their content.

These precautions, I think I took them to try and erase the traces of the film in order to keep the reader from using it instead of their own interpretation.

I believe now—surely I have always believed it—but how, how to occupy life?—that it was perhaps not worth the effort to make the film. I believe the film was no doubt surplus, too much, thus unnecessary, useless. That it was in sum the marriage of desire on the very premises of the night but of the night chased away, replaced by the day. The light in the bedroom of the lovers, I think it shouldn't have been done. After the writing of the text everything came too late, everything, because the event had already taken place, in fact, in the writing. Because writing, whether it be written or read, it's the same thing in this case, it's also the sharing of the general story. This story, which belongs to everyone, I had the right to have my part of it because that's how I share it with others, by writing. But perhaps I didn't have the right here—here, I think of evil, of the devil, of morality—once the writing was over, once that universal night of the abyss was penetrated and closed back up again, to act as if it were possible to go back there to look a second time. To pass through the abyss, that first age of men, of beasts, of fools, of the mud, through the specter of the light, even if it was through an identity that was uncontrollable, even accidental.

It was unavoidable to write *The Night*—we know this—yes, it was beyond control. But it was avoidable to film it—that we also know—and I won't get away with it: it was avoidable to make a film with that darkness. But how to occupy the time?

The person who is revealed in the abyss claims no identity. They claim only that, to be the same. The same as the person who answered them. As everyone. It's a fabulous clearing out that begins as soon as we dare to speak, rather as soon as we arrive there. Because as soon as we call we become, we are already the same. As who? As what? As what we know nothing about. And it's by becoming the same person that we leave the desert, society. To write is to be no one. "Dead," said Thomas Mann. When we write, when we call, already we are the same. Try. Try while you're alone in your bedroom, free, with no outside control, to call or to answer beyond the abyss.

To fuse with the vertigo, the immense flood of calls. This first word, this first shout, we don't know how to shout it. May as well call God. It's impossible. And it happens.

My good fortune is that I escaped from the first edit that I made. I wrote for the press, when the film was released, the story of that failure. I include it here for the sake of memory and also because I see it there already, albeit masked, the ban that I establish for myself, the film:

> "I began filming *The Ship Named Night* on Monday July 31, 1978. I had planned out the images. On the following Monday and Tuesday, through August 1st, I filmed the shots planned for the edit. Tuesday night, I saw Monday's rushes. In my journal that day, I wrote: *film ruined.*
>
> For one evening and one night, I abandoned the film, *The Night.* I stood outside of it, far, as separate from it as if it had never even existed. This had never happened to me before: to no longer see anything, no longer glimpse the slightest possibility of a film, of a single film frame. I had been completely wrong. The edit was false. More than that: I had been a stranger to the film: the edit didn't exist.
>
> I said to my friends: 'That's it, it happened to me.' My friends told me that it was normal, that given what I was trying to do in cinema, they had expected it. We spoke very little.

They had seen the rushes too and we were all in agreement. We spoke of what had to be done, notifying the production, the team, the actors, that everything would stop.

Benoît Jacquot told me to wait for the next morning to make a definitive decision about stopping the film. To sleep on it. I agreed.

I don't think I hoped for anything from that coming night, from sleep. It would have troubled me to keep hoping. I was happy, suddenly plunged into a boundless sterility, a kind of expanse without any accident, no suffering, nor desire. Finally present to myself in this assessment of an avowed failure, with no recourse. It was clear. It was finished.

Cinema, finished. I would start writing books again, I would return to my native land, to that terrifying labor that I had abandoned ten years prior. Meanwhile, I felt good. Happy. I had won that failure, I had won. The happiness must have stemmed from there, from having won. I leaned on that victory, that of having finally reached the impossibility of filming. I had never been so sure of a success as I was of that failure, that night.

I'll add that the financial aspect wasn't important to me. I gave myself permission to ruin a film, it didn't matter to me.

I slept. And then, as usual, I had that insomnia—a symptom of depression, they say—that comes before dawn. And during that insomnia I saw the disaster of the film. I saw the film.

In the morning, we met up again and I told my friends that we were going to abandon the edit and shoot the disaster of the film. During the day, we would film the set and the actors' makeup. We did it. Little by little, the film came back from the dead. I did it. I saw, each day a little more, that it was possible. I found the material to cover the screen while the sound, the story, elapsed. I realized that it was possible to attain a film derived from *The Night*, which would testify to the story all the more (but to an incalculable degree) than the supposed film of *The Night* that I had attempted for months never could have. We turned the camera around and we filmed what was going on inside, the night, the air, the projectors, some roads, some faces too."

The deferred narratives of *The Ship Named Night* about Greece are from episodes of the friendship that links us, Benoit Jacquot and me. It's true, I went to the Parthenon and to the Athens City Museum in that way. And it's also true that afterwards I recounted it to him alone. And also that then he went there strictly in the same way. It's our way of finding each other through time.

Cesarea and *Negative Hands* were written based on shots not used for *The Ship Named Night*. Then made with those shots.

The text titled *Aurélia Steine*r is followed by another text of the same title, *Aurélia Steiner.* A third text follows which also has that title. Two films were made based on the first two texts, which also have that title, *Aurélia Steiner.* For the sake of ease, we can call them, in the order of publication, by these titles: *Aurélia Melbourne*, *Aurélia Vancouver*, *Aurélia Paris.*

The Ship Named Night

— I told you it was something you had to see.
That around midday the silence over Athens becomes so… with the heat growing…The city empties around siesta time, everything closes like the night…

…that you had to witness the rising silence…

I remember, I said to you: little by little, you wonder what's happening, this disappearance of sound with the rising sun.

This is when the fear comes. Not a fear of the night, but something like the fear of night during the day. The silence of night in broad daylight. The sun at its peak and the silence of night. The silence at the center of the sky and the silence of night.

When the others arrived, around two in the afternoon, we went back down together to the city, Athens, and then nothing more happened.

Nothing.

Nothing except still, everywhere, that lack of love.

— At the Athens City Museum, that next afternoon…

— Oh yes… that's true... I'd forgotten… you know how it goes…

…and what I spoke of was the *other story*, the story of those other people…

— It's a Saturday. At night. In the springtime. It's almost the start of the summer. The month of June. He, the man in the story, is working.

He's on call in a telecommunications office.

He's bored.

Paris empties. The springtime. A Saturday. He's twenty-five years old. Alone.

He has access to certain numbers from the telephone abyss. He dials them. Two numbers. Three numbers.

— And then, there.

There she is.

The year is 1973.

He had a diary in those days and claims that he kept note of many things. But that after, he didn't. That he stopped. That he stopped not long after it started, this story, this love story.

A story without images.

A story of black images.

There, it begins.

She calls him at the same time as him in space and time.

They speak.

Speak.

— They describe themselves. She says she's a young woman with black hair. Long.

— He says he's also young, blonde, with very blue eyes, tall, almost thin, handsome.

— She talks to him about what she does. First she says that she works in a factory. Another time she says she's just returned from China. She tells him all about a trip to China.

— Yet another time she says she's studying medicine, in hopes of joining Doctors Without Borders.

— It seems that this is the version she stuck with thereafter. That she no longer changed it. That she never again said something other than the following: that she was finishing her studies in medicine, that she was a resident in a Paris hospital.

— He says she speaks eloquently. With ease. That you can't help but listen to her.
Believe her.

— He gives her his phone number. She, she doesn't give him hers.

— No, she doesn't.

— A month goes by.

It's during those days that she names herself. That she gives him a name he can call her, which starts with the letter F.

— He says she has the kind of voice anyone would love listening to. He says: rather fascinating.

— They speak. Tirelessly.

Speak.

— Endlessly describe themselves. One another. To one, the other. The color of their eyes. The grain of their skin. The softness of the breast held in the hand. The softness of that hand. At the very moment she speaks of this hand, she is looking at it. I see myself with your eyes.

— He says he sees.

Describes himself, now it's his turn.

He says he watches his own hand on his own body.

Says: it's the first time. Says what pleasure it brings, to be alone. Places the phone on his heart. Can she hear?

— She can hear.

— He says his entire body is also beating to the sound of her voice.

— She says that she knows. That she sees it. Hears it, eyes closed.

— He says: I was a stranger to myself and didn't know it.

— She says that before him she hadn't known she was desirable with a desire for herself that she herself could share.

And this is frightening.

— This story actually happened?

— Someone said they actually lived it, yes.

And then it was told by others.
And then it was drafted.
Written.

— It's at night that she calls.

— Yes, when night comes, she calls.

— When night is coming she comes.
"It's me F. I'm afraid."

— The conversations grow very long. Entire nights.

— They end up lasting until daytime. They last eight hours. Ten hours straight.

— He still doesn't know her name, her address, her phone number.

—He knows only this name that
she calls herself when he picks up the phone:

"It's me F. I'm afraid."

— He's at her disposal. He's the one who waits for the calls. He has no way of reaching her. No information about where she is.

— He doesn't ask for any. For months.

— One time she reveals certain things.

— One time she tells him: the place, Neuilly.
That's where she is, Neuilly.
A mansion.
Between the Seine and the Bois de Vincennes.

— Neuilly: Neuilly endlessly all around her…

— Around the black image…

— Neuilly endlessly all around her.

— Around the black image…

— For nights and nights they live on the phone. They sleep against the receiver. Speak or go quiet. Make each other come.

— It's a black orgasm. With no reciprocal touching.
Nor a face. Eyes closed.
Your voice, only.
The text of the voices said with eyes closed.

— No image on the text of desire?

— Which image?

— I don't see what it could be.

— So there is nothing to see.

— Nothing. No image.
The ship named Night faces an eternal night.

— Blind, advances.
On the sea of black ink.

— The ship named Night has just entered its story.

— She is the first to want to see him, meet him.

She sets two kinds of meetings. Those which are canceled. Those which are not.

He goes to every meeting.

Each time there are unforeseen circumstances which render their meeting impossible.

He's not surprised by the impediments
to their meeting.
He finds them believable, each time.

— He believes what she says.
Believes her.

— Very quickly, he can do nothing to deviate the story. It is she F. who leads the story. Pits herself against it. Avoids recklessness.

— Who little by little makes them both grow accustomed to it.
She, she knows nothing. Invents.
The first to go crazy.

— Months pass.

A year.

— Three years.

—The story digs itself caverns, deepens. The more its setting expands, the darker it gets.

— One day she tells him: she's sick. Leukemia. Sentenced to death. Alive now because of treatments, money, for the last ten years, since the age of sixteen. She is now twenty-six years old.

—All around her, the filthy Seine.

—And that Bois de Vincennes.
Those sad surroundings
Plagued also
With death.

—There's a period when she refuses to see him. Refuses the idea. She says that they will never meet. That they will never see one another.

— She says that she loves him like crazy. That she is crazy in love with him. That she would leave it all behind for him.

Out of love for you, I would leave behind my family, the house in Neuilly.
But this does not mean that we should see one another.
I could leave it all behind for you without ever joining you.

Leave it all behind because of you, for you, and yet never join anything.
Invent this faithfulness to our love.

She says that she loves him like crazy. That she is crazy in love with him. That she would leave it all behind for him.

Out of love for you, I would leave behind my family, the house in Neuilly.

But this does not mean that we should see one another.

I could leave it all behind for you without ever joining you.

Leave it all behind because of you, for you, and yet never join anything.

Invent this faithfulness to our story.

— This insomniac land of Paris at night, it's the sea upon which the Night passes. This film. This ship adrift that they've named: Night.

In the day, nothing is seen of this passage of night.

In the day, nothing.

The movements of the ship named Night should testify to other movements happening elsewhere and of a different nature.

The movements of the ship named Night should testify to the movements of desire.

— He insists. He wants to see.

Because the idea of seeing scares him more and more, he wants to see.

As a way to liquidate the story, to put an end to it.

— They both know that the distance is no longer measurable between the one who cries out at night, fused with the generality of desire, the one disfigured by the abyss, and the other—who would she be?—whom he would not recognize by sight, whom he would only recognize eyes closed in the darkness of the world.

— He does not promise to close his eyes as she approaches, decent, covered with a white Chanel scarf at the corner of rue de Neuilly.

No he did not promise not to look.

— She concedes.
A meeting is set.

— Paris, July 1973.

— On an intensely hot day.

Their meeting should take place in a café on Place de Bastille at three in the afternoon.

— He waits for her, for an hour and a half he says.
Probably even longer.
She does not come.

That night, she calls. She says that she went to the meeting. That she saw him.

— That he was wearing a light summer shirt. She describes its color. Its transparency.
She says that she wasn't able to stop.

— He saw nothing pass by him that resembled her black image, the one she gave him on the first day.

She passed by him in a car. Behind her, her father's chauffeur followed, as ordered by her father. That's what she will say. That she had obtained from this father the permission to see him on the condition that she didn't stop.

— The chauffeur had admitted to her that he had

received the order to make sure she obeyed the father. And so she couldn't have stopped without compromising the chauffeur. Does he understand?

— He understands.

— From then on, she can no longer forget this man she saw, who was awaiting this woman, her. The body she glimpsed through the transparency of the shirt, as she passed by, that dark trace of the nipples on the thin chest fill her with madness.

— She, she has seen him now. A few seconds. But the image is there forever.

I'm not speaking about the image of your face but of your body.

— It occurs to him that she was forbidden on that day of such great heat, and because of the leukemia, to leave the car and walk towards him.

Or that it was from an ambulance rented for that reason—to see him—that she saw him awaiting her.

After the meeting at Place de Bastille, she enters desire each time, each night.

Each night demands to die of it.
Asks to die of it.

—The people who cry at night into the abyss all set meetings. These meetings never end in encounters. They're just set.

— It's the call that is hurled down the abyss, the cry, which unleashes the orgasm.

— It's the other cry. The response.

— Someone cries. Someone responds that they've heard the cry, that they're responding to it.

It's this response that sets off the agony.

—You say that you remember this man who shouted at dawn.

—Yes. He called. He said he was the Cat. I'm the Cat… Do you hear? The Cat is calling… This is the Cat…

— His tone was an order.

— He gave orders, yes. But he also begged.

— He said the Cat was seeking someone.

That the Cat wanted to orgasm.

That someone had to answer.

— It was a man who answered. The voice was very sweet, tender. He said he could hear the Cat. That he was answering to say this, that he could hear him.

— He told him to come. To orgasm.

Come. Orgasm.

—Yes.

The voice of the Cat subsided in sobs.
It was in Paris in winter around four o'clock, in the middle of the night.

— Another time. Yet another time she gives him new information: she has two mothers. She's an illegitimate child. Her official mother is not her real mother.

— Her real mother is a former maid from the mansion in Neuilly. She's now retired. She lives in the suburbs.

— She's under surveillance.

Those around her worry about these very long phone calls, at night, because they tire her so greatly.

Orders are given by the father that the damage to F.'s health be limited to these phone calls.

— So that nothing further would take place. Nothing beyond these phone calls.

— The father's chauffeur is the first to warn her of this surveillance. He too, this chauffeur, wants her to be well, to survive, like everyone else around her.

— One day.
One day the Neuilly house slips away.

He thinks the whole thing is a lie. He no longer believes someone is dying there.

Although he can still see the Neuilly house, this ship adrift paused between the hedges, he no longer sees someone dying there.

For him it no longer contains the legend of this sole heiress with the unknown name, leukemic and illegitimate. The one he desires.

— He suddenly doubts one of the terms F. has given him, the illness. He says that it's simply too much. He speaks of a strategy. He tells her that she's lying.

That she's lying.

— So she speaks of the irrefutable proof of her leukemia. That blonde hair she has, very long, very beautiful, an enormous mass, surprising, which she sleeps in. If only he could see.

— She's surprised. How can he not know such a common, known thing?… that leukemia makes your hair grow very long, very beautiful, and blonde beyond compare?

— He reminds her that the first night she described herself as a brunette.

She says that he didn't hear her correctly.

He does not resist.

— The dates get scrambled.
The diary is no longer kept as regularly.
The timeline is no longer certain.

— What's left is a global memory of the event.
So thorough, that every night testifies to the totality of desire.

— Walls fall between the days.

— She says that she's suffering. Physically. A lot. More and more. That she's very feeble. More and more feeble. So feeble that she falls, and often. And that she hurts herself, and that her entire body is marked with the marks and wounds of her falls.

— And that her pleasure is all mixed up with this pain.

— She says: the illness is getting worse, it's growing. She says that she continues her work in the Parisian hospital where she's doing her residency. But that she's more frequently confined to her bed, on a drip. That she is only alive because of these infusions, these transfusions.

And then, sometimes, suddenly, she's reborn, lives once more.

— This balance between life and death.
Disappears
Dies
Quiets

And then comes back to life
He says that he starts to love her.

— That's when the Neuilly house becomes frightened.

He receives phone calls from the father's wife, the illegitimate mother. She knows the number of the young man from Les Gobelins.

He will never know if F. is the one who gave her this number or if it was stolen as she slept.

The illegitimate mother begs him to leave F. alone. Says that these nights on the phone exhaust her child, kill her. That this child's life hangs in the balance.

— He asks: how, in what way could he leave her alone? He himself has no way to call her, he knows neither her address, nor her name, nor her phone number.

The illegitimate mother says that he could refuse to answer her.

— So he does. Cuts the communication the moment he recognizes her voice.

— She calls back.
She disguises her voice.
He recognizes it.
And once more does not resist.
Answers her.

— One day, a woman comes to his house to bring him an envelope from F. She says she's the linen keeper in the Neuilly house. Perhaps the chauffeur's wife.

— The envelope contains two photographs.
It's a young woman.
She has blonde hair, very long, very beautiful.
She's rather tall. Thin.
He says: her face is banal.

— She is photographed in a garden. A lawn between trees and hedges.

— The envelope also contains a handkerchief embroidered with her initials and a sum of money in bills.

— The story stops with the photographs.

— Alone at night, with these unrecognizable photographs. Locked up with them. Desperate.

— The ship named Night is stopped on the sea.
It no longer has a route. An itinerary.

— Desire is dead, killed by an image.

— He can no longer answer the phone. He's afraid.
After the photographs he would no longer recognize her voice.
Who is it, so unpredictable?
Who?
It's too late for her to have a face.

He must return these photographs. Quick.
He does not know how to return them. Nor to whom.
Then he remembers.

— He remembers. The linen keeper who brought him the envelope said she was in contact with F.'s real mother. She said they both lived in the same housing project on the outskirts of Paris.

— The linen keeper, by order of F., gave him her personal phone number.
Mademoiselle told me to give you my phone number, here it is, you never know.

— A divide is crossed.
The real mother calls him. "What can I do for you, sir?"
He says he wants to return the photographs.
She doesn't ask which photographs.
She says fine.
The meeting is set. He will go to her place.

— It's a housing project near Vincennes. An apartment bought by the father as a reward for the child.
She's the one who answers the door.

— Sixty years old. The look of a maid. That's what he says, she has the look of a maid. Alone on the thirteenth floor. A view of the eastern suburbs. Vincennes-Saint-Mandé. Exile.

— The apartment is working class. European-finish plywood furniture. A faux fur on the bed. The immaculate cleanliness of the void.

— A smooth face, absent gaze. She takes the photographs without a word. He does not ask who this woman in the garden is. Young. Blonde. She does not tell him. Does not ask why he returns them.

He asks her to tell him about F.

She says that she had F. before the father's marriage with the other woman, the one who bears the name of the father. That after this marriage, she was hired as the child's nanny in the Neuilly house.

— Then when the child was grown she was kept on as a maid. This, still out of kindness, she says, so she would not be separated from her child, all that she has in this world.

He will never know anything about the relationship between F. and her real mother.

It's only later, it seems, when she was already grown, that F. learnt her real mother was the one who slept in the basement of the Neuilly house.

— That the woman who had been loved by her father, the only woman, was this one.

— He will see the real mother again several times. By order of her child she will return to see him to bring other gifts, other sums of money.

— The linen keeper too, like the real mother, goes to see him by order of the young mistress of Neuilly. They come to deliver envelopes containing money and gifts.

— A golden lighter. A lizard-skin wallet. But that's not the main thing.

— The main thing is the money.

They will never come to his home without a large sum of money.

He takes the money.

For him, the sums of money are significant.

— She speaks of giving him everything. Of giving him a car, an apartment. Everything.

— She will no longer give him photographs, whether they are of other women or herself.

Those photographs are never mentioned between them.

The photographs of that young woman in the garden will never be mentioned.

She has never brought them up.

— He says: I forgot the photographs.

It started up like before.

— What's the money for? What does it buy? The love story perhaps? Something is bought in this story. There must be a price to pay for something in this story.

— He takes the money, therefore confirming the payment.

— No doubt the money works here as elsewhere, as always, in its salary function.

— Always delivered by the same hands. Here, these, the hands of the young mistress of Neuilly.

She pays him for giving her so much pleasure.

— I had told you that I left the hotel well before the others, that I'd arrived there around eleven in the morning. That I was alone. Except for two ladies from the French and American embassies whom I saw at the Athens airport, alone.

That I had remained there until two in the afternoon.

You came the same way, right?

—Yes.

— I told you it was something you had to see. See.

That around midday the silence over Athens becomes so... with the growing heat... The city empties around siesta time, everything closes like the night...

I spoke to you of terror.

I said to you: little by little, you wonder *w*hat's happening... this disappearance of sound with the rising sun...

This is when the fear comes.

Not a fear of the night, but something like the fear of night during the day... the silence of night in broad daylight... the sun at its peak and the silence of the night... fear...

And so the shade glides and accumulates at the feet of the columns, it amasses, hardens, and for a moment, there is no shade at all. As if hidden, you see?

Disappeared...

The silence is such that it reverts to that of the countryside. A calm valley.

...so much so that a swarm of butterflies made a mistake. The swarm traversed the silence, the abyss of the city. It arrived on the hill. It traversed the temple.

It came from Attica.

They were white.

It's at that moment I saw. As the butterflies were making their crossing, I saw... the temple was not white but made of blue marble.

And then, shade, it returns.

It erects the temple once more on the side opposite its disappearance.

Like a black line at first.

And then like a stroke.

You are less afraid.

The relief can be seen once more.

Little by little the entire beach along the temple has been covered with darkness.

When the others arrived, around two in the afternoon, they visited the temple. Then we went back down together to the city. Athens.

And then nothing more happened. Nothing more.

Nothing. Nothing except still, everywhere, those cries. That same lack of love.

— At the Athens City Museum, that next afternoon...

— Oh yes that's true... I'd forgotten... you know how it goes... yes... and it just so happened to be the same day... I spoke to you of the other story... the story of those other people...[1]

— *At first, he finds nothing in common between F. and her mother. Then suddenly, when the mother calls him to announce she will be bringing him a gift, he finds their voices alike. The inflection of their voices. When she calls him, he confuses them. Often.*

---

1. In the film *Le Navire Night*, this part of the text was abandoned. A fragment of it was kept for the beginning of the film.

— It's her, the real mother, who calls. He can only reach her through the linen keeper, the chauffeur's wife.

— He asks her several times to give him her daughter's number. She doesn't refuse.

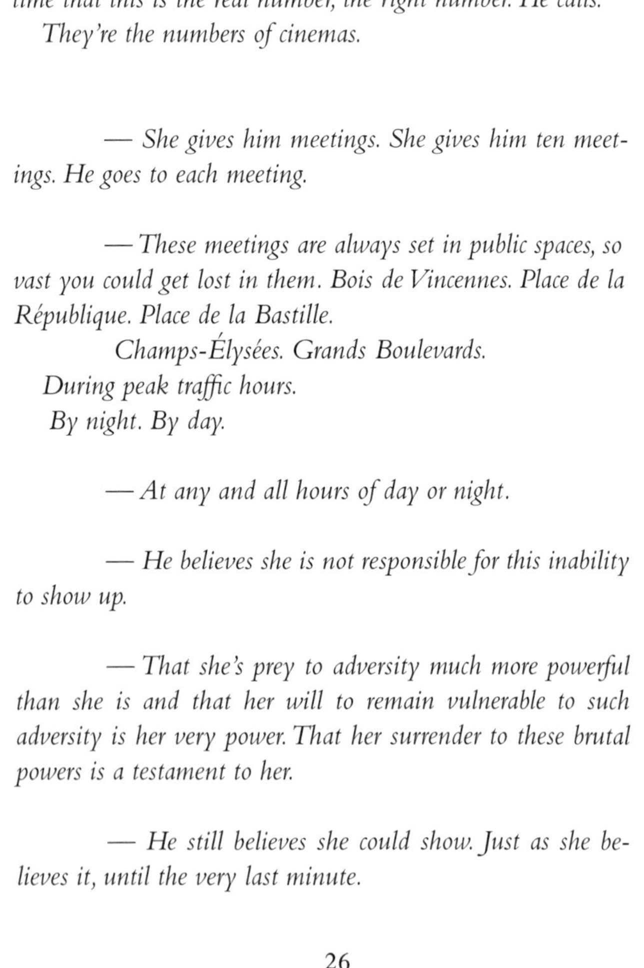

— She gives him a number each time. Says each time that this is the real number, the right number. He calls.

They're the numbers of cinemas.

— She gives him meetings. She gives him ten meetings. He goes to each meeting.

— These meetings are always set in public spaces, so vast you could get lost in them. Bois de Vincennes. Place de la République. Place de la Bastille.

Champs-Élysées. Grands Boulevards.

During peak traffic hours.

By night. By day.

— At any and all hours of day or night.

— He believes she is not responsible for this inability to show up.

— That she's prey to adversity much more powerful than she is and that her will to remain vulnerable to such adversity is her very power. That her surrender to these brutal powers is a testament to her.

— He still believes she could show. Just as she believes it, until the very last minute.

He says: and anyway, surely, she can't manage to get herself out of it. That thickness. That Forest.

— She speaks of the father.
She speaks of the money.
Often.
The father. Fearsome and venerated. Venerated by all. Feared by all. Quite a situation. Director of the State's major financial body. Private financial advisor to the President of the French Republic. He's the money purveyor.
The money seems infinite. Laughable.

— A property in Lago Maggiore.

— Another in Sainte-Marie in Provence.

— Another in Bormes-les-Mimosas.

— And this house here, in Neuilly.

— The sole heiress, she, F., the child sentenced to death.

— The father.
He, the father, never calls. He makes his threats through the Neuilly house women. The story cannot exist beyond the confines of those phone calls.

— He thinks the story will be less damaging to F. if it's invisible.

That the father is so out of step with his daughter is a testament to the father. To his fundamental handicap when it comes to desire.

— Once, on a daytime phone call, he hears someone call a name in the house that she responds to. It's the illegitimate mother calling her child.

This is how he learns her Christian name and marital status.

— She does not deny it.

From now on, he will call her by this name.

— The father's name, her last name, that one, she says it's up to him to figure it out.

That there are different kinds of research he can undertake. Secondary research. And primary research.

— The primary research should take place in Père-Lachaise Cemetery.

She tells him how, how to reach the place of primary research. It's there, in a corner of the temple of death. The site is not visited often. The stones are green. Monumental. Unearthed. Unreadable for the most part.

— There lies the dumpster of Empire marshals en-

nobled on the great sites of death at the turn of the nineteenth century, of Dukes of Dalmatia and Austerlitz, of France and Waterloo, of the descendants of a debauched line of dubious financiers, of Neuilly riffraff who emigrated out of fear of the Paris Commune, and of the mishmash of their women and children.

— It's there, in that dumpster, that you must search. Her mother's maiden name can also be found there. As a descendant of the great military leaders of the Napoleon Army and the financiers of that reign, she's there too, in that junkyard.

— But it's also in that same junkyard, fused with her, that her paternal grandfather's name can be found. Thus, the name of her father. Thus, her own.

— She doesn't explain why, even before their birth, the names of her mother and father find themselves already wedded on the tombstones of Père-Lachaise.

Misalliances no doubt subsequently corrected by these marriages? We don't know.

— The explanation is lost.

— He does not go to Père-Lachaise.

— But she, she thinks that he has, that he's done the research she asked.

There's an entire period when she believes he knows who she is based on this name. That with this name he will be able to find the Neuilly house.

— He doesn't tell her that he never went to Père-Lachaise.

— I had told you where she was, between two halls, the last of this vast city museum, just before the hall with the copper horse carcasses that were found in 1960, in the Port of Piraeus.

It was because of that wound on her face, I think, that I was so utterly struck by her. That wound contrasted with the gaze… unbroken, you see… I can't remember exactly.

I stared at her a long time.

You didn't find her in the museum?

— No.

— Her name is written.

— Athena.

— Yes, that's it…

She must have had the left side of her face torn off by a plowshare, by iron, but her eyes are intact… white almonds without relief of any kind...

The work has never been reproduced?

— Never.

— The head is so little, it could fit in one hand. I had told you the head of a child.

It's on a low column lost between the tall steles, the mishmash of the last halls.

Actually, it's possible that finding it trivial, and precisely because of that wound, the Museum's authorities have stored it in the underground storage.

But what surprises me is that this would have happened between my visit and yours, in the same day…

— Why not?

— It's true… Why not…

— The wound on the face is terrible. It must be largely responsible for the depth of the gaze.

— That gaze is for you…

— Yes, that's it, it's a gaze that gazes at you… it gazes at the one who gazes but also right through them… and even further than that… beyond the end, to those far-off lands… you see… we just can't… we just don't know which names to give them… they're common to all of history…

— I see without seeing.

— Yes, that's it.

— The next day, we left Athens, and then
nothing more happened.
Nothing more.
Except, still, everywhere, those cries.
That same lack of love.

— In Paris.
In Paris, love, still. At night. A dead end.
Pleasure in sobs.
Between them, that insurmountable wall, blind.

— Sometimes they cannot do without each other. They call each other by night, by day.

— Sometimes they can no longer stand each other.
They fight.
Shout.
Separate.

— And one day, jealousy erupts.

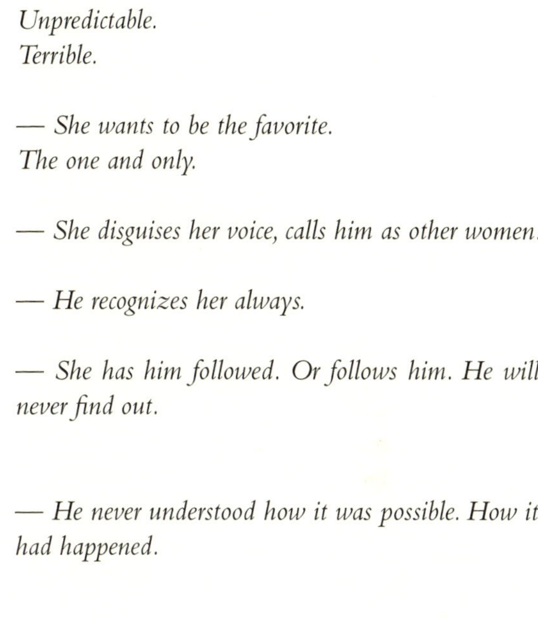

Unpredictable.
Terrible.

— She wants to be the favorite.
The one and only.

— She disguises her voice, calls him as other women.

— He recognizes her always.

— She has him followed. Or follows him. He will never find out.

— He never understood how it was possible. How it had happened.

— In the evening, she calls him, she tells him the hour he left work, the places he went to, the streets he bikes down before going home.

All his routes.

— He doesn't want to look behind him. He knows. He knows he's trapped under surveillance at every instant.

— He doesn't want to find out who's there, behind him.

She provokes him into the game of death. He plays this game like he could never have predicted.

They both know: if he turns around and sees who it is, the story dies off, is struck down.

— He knows, it's her. The details given every evening on the phone cannot fool him.

"And when you took rue du Val-de-Grâce, the sun came out and you looked at the sky..."

— He arrives home. Rushes into the building corridor. He knows: she's there, watches him disappear. He doesn't turn around. He waits, wild with a desire that brings him to tears.

— It's during this time that he discovers the phenomenal power of solitude, the unaddressed violence of desire.

— It's at this moment that he refuses the mortal story so as to remain in the universal abyss.

— He says now that he never saw anyone follow him.

— He says also that he noticed, once, a chauffeur-driven car stopped near his workplace. Empty.

— Once, when she calls him from the depths of the Neuilly evening silence, he hears a man's voice asking Madame "if he can clear the table." She has not lied about the wealth, there's a butler at the Neuilly house.

— That trip to Saône-et-Loire.
He had told her that this is where he was born. She goes there, travels through the region until she finds the house.

Finds it. Describes it perfectly upon her return. Also finds the apartment of his mother in a neighboring town. Calls her, tells her that she is crazy in love with him, her child.

— Does he know if she's still alive?

— He says no, nothing.

— Can he find out?

— He could call the linen keeper, that other woman from the projects. But he can't do it now. He no longer has her number. He no longer remembers her name. He can't request that information.

— According to him, is she dead?

— He says: maybe, that he doesn't know, no idea… But… probably… yes… she was so sick at the end.

— At the end?

— Yes, when it stopped.

— She had made the decision several times to stop calling him.
Then once she went through with it.

— Once she went through with it.

If she's dead, her grave is at Père-Lachaise. In that case it would be easy to tell, by the freshness of the tombstone and of the stirred earth, it would be easy to tell that it's her.

— The name, in that case, which would be followed by the first name, written last, would be hers.

— He says: I was crazy. We were crazy.

— Crazy with what: with desire for her?

— He says he's not sure exactly what he was crazy with. That he could not have been crazy for her, with desire for her. How could that have been possible?

— With the image?

— With desire itself?

— He answers that he doesn't know.

— Did she exist?

— Who? Who would not have existed?

He says: Yes, she existed. In any case. She existed. Whoever she was, whoever she might still be, she existed.

Exists.

— Wherever she came from, whatever alibi she maintained, she existed. She exists.

Even if she were that sixty year-old woman from the Vincennes projects, she would exist. He says the question is unfounded.

— Three years.

— The number of hours spent on the phone: months.

— There are periods, sometimes a month long, during which she gives no sign of life. Perhaps she's too sick to do so during those periods.

— And then she calls once more.

The joint orgasm is arid.
Immense
Exposed
Incomparable.

— One night, he asks her: did she have lovers before him? Had a man approached her? All he has of her is that smell of the bills that have been touched by her hands.

— She says yes. She had a lover. A priest she met on a train. She made him crazy with love.

Then she left him.

She gives him all the details. She shouts the details.

— Their pleasure culminates in murder. She shouts while recounting the torment of the crazy-in-love priest she had left.

He shouts that he wants to know more.

— At dawn they find themselves once more in separate beds. They cry.

— Towards the end, she's almost always lying down, dying. She's continuously on a drip. Sometimes she faints on the phone.

— He knows by the sound of her voice. He can tell her voices apart. Her lying down voice.

Her dying voice.

Her trapped voice, her child's voice.

— Her voice when she speaks of the beloved father. Her gossip voice, her liar voice.

— Her distorted voice, detuned with desire.

— Her terrified voice.
She can no longer lie to him.

— One more time. She gives him a clue about the Neuilly house. Right now they're building a fountain in the garden. Between the hedge and the lawn. For an entire day he roams the streets of Neuilly on a bicycle. A whole day. He doesn't look for the fountain in the garden, but something else. An unexpected but conclusive detail.

The color of a wall. Of a gate.

— A singular layout of bedroom windows. A singular veiled light over everything. A sign from the heavens.

— He finds nothing. He says that he did not roam through every street in Neuilly.

— That next day he starts over.
She lets him search.
Gives no additional clue.

— Except for this one however, on the night of that day, that her room is visible from the street, that the windows are never closed, that her bed is thus exposed to all gazes.

— He says now that he could have found the Neuilly house had he wanted to see.

— Did he have an image of her?

— He says that in the beginning, yes, he would have had that black image, of the woman with black hair. And that later this image must have been replaced by the one in the two photographs. And that later still, when the photographs had been forgotten, he must have recovered that black image she gave him.

He says he no longer has any image of her now.

— Does he say he has lied?

— No. He says he must have mixed up some mo-

ments, some days, some places, that he has no timeline—that he has no clear reason for this, that he sees no use for one.

He says that she, same as him, would have mistaken her own image in the mirror for the one of the young man glimpsed at Place de Bastille. Life for death. Her own body for his, so unknown. His own body's unknown for each and every unknown.

That she, same, same as him, would not have known whether she was the one from the story or the one, outside of it, who was watching the story.

— He says that she was perhaps that young child who, on those nights she claimed to be unwell, went beneath the windows and watched her die.

— That young Neuilly prowler who went at night and watched her die.

— At one point she goes several days without calling. When she starts to call again she tells him the news.

— She says she's getting sicker and sicker. She will die.

Announces her wedding.

— Her husband is that surgeon who has been caring for her the last ten years. Does he remember? The one who has known her forever, who saw her come into the world? Who has always cared for her, protected her?

— Not long after someone calls. A man. He claims to be her future husband. He demands that they put an end to their relationship.

He confirms her imminent death.

— He pronounces for the first time the word crazy.

— For the first time the word is pronounced: crazy.

— She calls one last time.

— Tells him the date of the wedding. Not the place.

— Says she has only ever felt love for him, her only lover.

Regrets having to die.

— The wedding takes place on a summer day, in 1975. Not in Paris.

—You spoke of the sea also.

— Oh yes, maybe… Of the dead rats along the docks of Thessaloniki… of the smell of anise, of ouzo… of the smell of the sludge too… of the end of the sea.

—You spoke of a film also.

—Yes… the film… the film was never shot… There would have been people here. They would have been found here, immersed in a very absorbing common reflection…

— And that suddenly would have come to a halt… or would have been halted by death for example…

—That's it, yes… or by a sudden doubt… of a general nature.

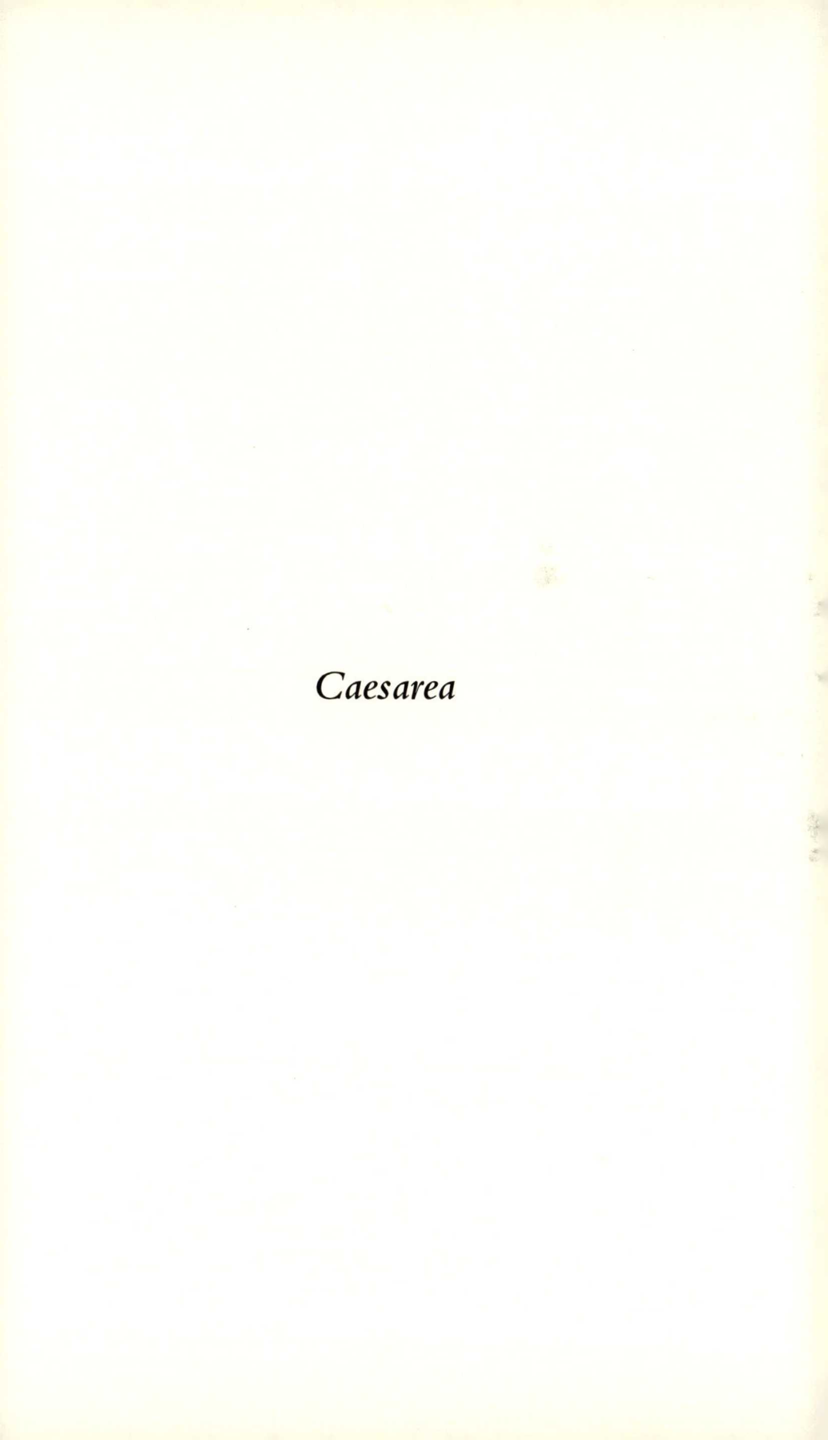

Caesarea

Césarée
Césarée
That's what this place is called
Césarée
Caesarea

Nothing remains of it but the memory of history
and this sole word to name it
Césarée
The totality.
Nothing but the place
And the word.

The ground.
It's white.
Marble dust
mixed with sand from the sea.

Despair.
Intolerable.
The despair of their separation.

Césarée.
The place is still called.
Césarée
Caesarea.

The place is flat
facing the sea
The sea is at the end of its run
strikes the ruins
still strong
there, now, facing the other continent already.
Blue from the blue marble columns cast there in front of the port.

All destroyed.
All was destroyed.

Césarée
Caesarea.
Captured.
Taken away.
Brought into exile on the Roman ship,
the queen of the Jews,
the woman queen of Samaria.
By him.

Him.
The criminal
The one who had destroyed the temple of Jerusalem.

And then she was repudiated.

The place is still called
Césarée
Caesarea.

The end of the sea
The sea that thumps against the deserts

Nothing is left but the history
The whole.
Nothing but that marble rubble under foot
That dust.
And the blue of the drowned columns.

The sea reached the land of Césarée.
The streets of Césarée were narrow, dark.
Their coolness gave way to the sun in places
the arrival of ships
and the dust of herds.
In that dust
we still see, we still read the thought
of the people of Césarée
the outline of the streets of the populations of Césarée.

Her, the queen of the Jews.
Returned there.
Repudiated.
Chased out
For the sake of public interest
Repudiated for the sake of public interest
Returns to Césarée.
The voyage across the sea in that Roman ship.
Struck down by the intolerable despair of having left him, the criminal of the temple.

Down in the ship she rests in slips of white mourning cloth.
The news of her despair erupts and spreads over the world.
The news crosses the seas, spreads over the world.

The place is called Césarée.

Caesarea.

In the north, Lake Tiberias, the great caravanserai of Saint-Jean-d'Acre.
Between the lake and the sea, Judea, Galilee.
All around, fields of banana trees, corn, orange groves
the wheats of Galilee.
To the south, Jerusalem, to the East, Asia, the deserts.

She was very young, eighteen, thirty, two thousand years old.
He took her there.
Repudiated for the sake of public interest
The Senate spoke of the danger of such a love.

Snatched from him.
From his desire.
Fatally.

In the morning, in front of the city, the Roman ship.
Silent, white as chalk, appears.
With no shame.

In the sky suddenly the eruption of ash
Over the towns called Pompeii, Herculaneum

Dead.
Destroys everything
Fatally.

The place is called Césarée
Caesarea
There is nothing left to see. Except for the whole.

In Paris it's a dreary summer.
Cold. Hazy.

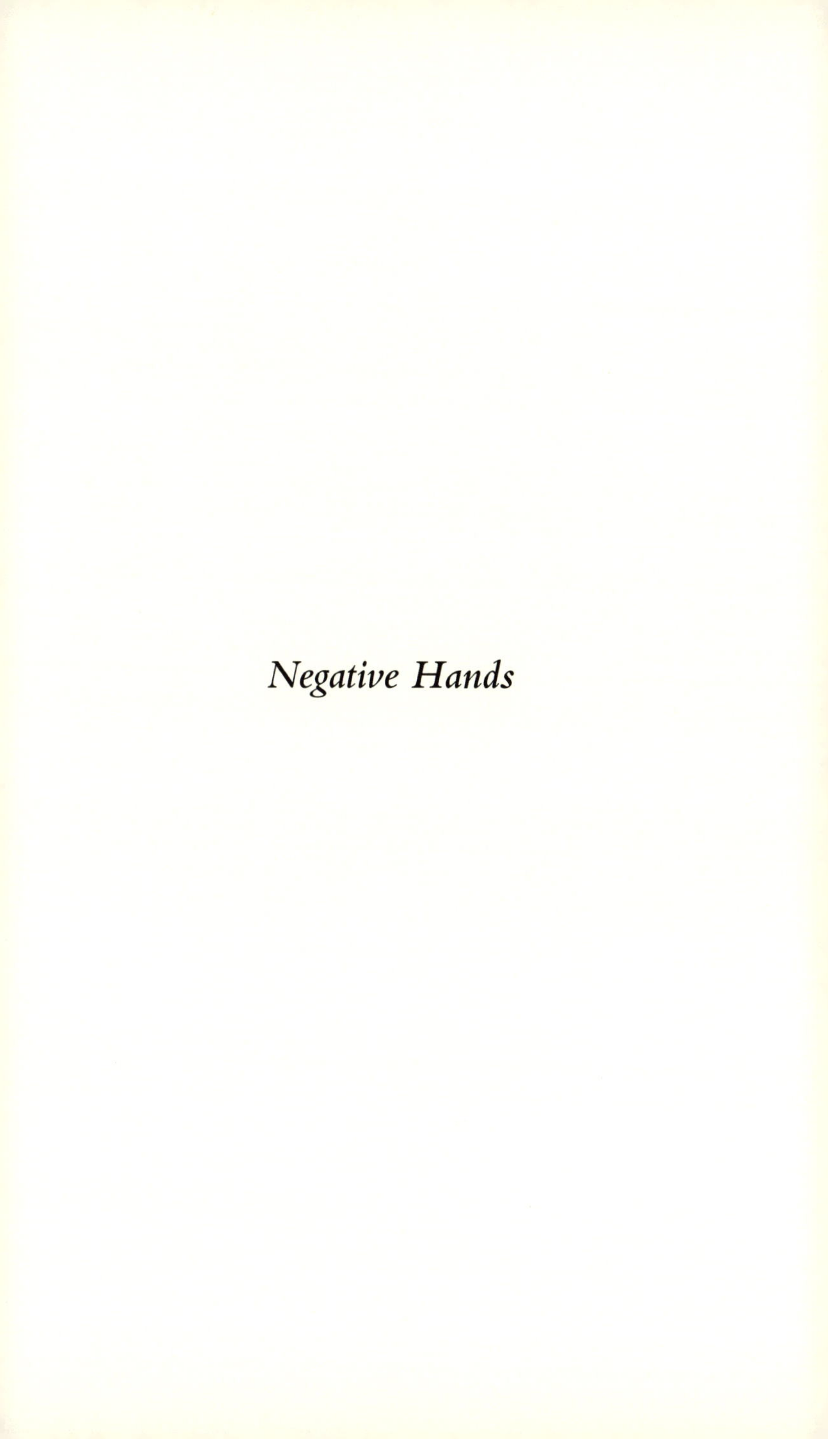

Negative Hands

The term *negative hands* is used to describe the hand paintings found in the Magdalenian caves in Subatlantic Europe. The outline of these hands—spread wide open on the rock—was coated with pigment. Most often blue, black. Sometimes red. No explanation has been found for this practice.

Before the ocean
under the cliff
on the granite wall

these hands

open

Blue
And black

The blue of the water
The black of the night

The man came alone into the cave
facing the ocean
All the hands are the same size
he was alone

The man alone in the cave saw
amid the sound
amid the sound of the sea
the immensity of things

And he shouted

You who have a name you who possess an identity I love you

These hands
the blue of the water
the black of the sky

Flat

Spread wide over the gray granite

So that someone would see them

I am the one who calls
I am the one who called who shouted thirty thousand years ago

I love you

I shout that I want to love you, I love you

I will love anyone who hears me shout

On the empty earth these hands will remain on the granite wall facing the roar of the ocean

Unbearable

No one will hear anymore

Will see

Thirty thousand years
Those hands, black

The refraction of the light on the sea makes the stone wall tremble

I am someone I am the one who called who shouted in that white light

Desire

the word is not yet invented

He saw the immensity of things in the roar of the waves, the immensity of his strength

and then he shouted

Above him the forests of Europe,
endless

He stands in the center of the rock
corridors
stone paths
from every direction

You who have a name you who possess an identity I love you with an indefinite love

Descend the cliff
vanquish fear

The wind blows from the continent it rebuffs
the ocean
The waves battle against the wind
They advance
slowed by its strength
and patiently reach
the wall

Everything crashes

I love you beyond you
I will love anyone who hears me shout that I love you

Thirty thousand years

I call

I call the one who will answer me

I want to love you I love you

For thirty thousand years I have been shouting before the sea,
the white ghost

I am the one who shouted that he loved you, you

Aurélia Steiner
(Aurélia Melbourne)

I write to you all the time, always this, you see.
Nothing other than this. Nothing.

Perhaps I will write you a thousand letters, give you letters about my life now.

And you, you would do with them what I would like you to do with them, which is whatever you like.

That's what I desire. For this to be addressed to you.

Where are you?

How to reach you?

How to bring us closer to this love together, overturn this apparent fragmentation of time that separates us from each other?

It's three in the afternoon.

Behind the trees is the sun, it's cold out.

I'm in that large room where I stay in the summer, facing the garden. On the other side of the windows is that forest of roses and, for the last three days, this cat, skinny, white, that comes to watch me through the windows, eye to eye, it scares me, it cries out, it's lost, it wants to belong, and I don't want to anymore.

Where are you?

What are you doing?

Where are you lost?

Where are you lost while I cry out I'm afraid?

They say that you live on one of those islands off the coast of France, and other places too.

They say you're in a tropical land where you died a long time ago, in the heat, buried in the mass graves of a plague, in the mass grave of another war also, and also in one at a camp in German-occupied Poland.

For me it's all the same.

I see your eyes.

I see that the sky of the river is blue, the same liquid blue color of your eyes.

I see that it's not true.
That when I write to you no one is dead.
And that you too are here, in this deserted continent.

Here it's summer.

Did you like summer?
I don't know anymore.

I also don't know if I liked it anymore.

I also don't know if I liked it outside of you.

Do you remember?

This word. This country. This dark land.

You said: There's nothing left but that path there.
That river.

How to get back to our love. How?

The light dips behind the trees, it seems.
There is wind. It must be getting colder.

The garden is full of birds and the cat grows wild with hunger.

The roses will die very soon now. It will get dark on the other side of the windows.

The sky, above the river, will turn black.

Night is falling.

Over this leprous and hungry cat, terrifying, over this motionless garden all around it, the night falls too. I see it.

It spreads over you, over me, over the river.

Can you still see?

They say that everything had been constructed on this earth.

That everything had been inhabited, occupied, by peoples, governments.

That there were palaces on the banks of rivers and, between the palaces, thickets of stinging nettle, bramble bushes and throngs of children running about. Women, skinny.

That there were islands.

Temples.

That there was a forest.

I don't know any general knowledge about peoples and the world.

None of them will take the place of you, of this fondness I have for you. None.

Listen,

under the arches of the river, there is now the sound of the sea.

Those of the black cave.

Those of the cries of the leprous cat, you know, the one blinded by hunger and calling through time.

Do you hear it?

No?

You don't hear anything anymore, perhaps?

No?

Listen again. Try. Try again.

How to conquer our love?

Listen.

Under the arches of the river, that surging.

Listen...

That apparent fragmentation I spoke to you about, has disappeared.

We must approach the end together.

That of our love.

Don't be afraid.

It's strange, the appearance the river takes on sometimes in the glow of the night, as if going towards the sea very quickly to completely dissolve within it...

But who are you?

Who?

How can it happen?

How will it be done?

In London, during that plague? You think so?

Or this war?

In the camp in East Germany?

In the one in Siberia? Or on these islands, here?

Here, you think?

No?

Me, I don't know anymore.

I know only this love that I have for you. Complete. Terrible.

And that you are not here to release me from it.

Never. Never will I separate you from our love.
From your story, your history.

They killed people here.

Did you know that?

Killed, yes.

Nearly every day. For a thousand years. A thousand and a thousand years.

Yes. Once. A thousand times. A hundred thousand.

The river full of blood.

They drew blood, they imprisoned, they wounded.

A thousand years.

It was then, yes, after, that this happened.

For a very, very long time, nothing.

And then, once, your eyes.

Your eyes on me.

First the liquid and empty blue of your eyes.

And then, you saw me.

All around that skinny wild cat, night has fallen now.

All around me, your form.

They say that it's in those crematoriums, you know, near Krakow, that your body was separated from mine… as if that were possible…

They say nonsense… they know nothing…

Listen…

The cat. It's crying…

Hunger and the wind devour it in the black garden…

Listen…

Through its tears, the cat…

From the wind and hunger, it cries. In the black cave…

Listen…

Its cries… Like moans… As if it were speaking…

Listen…

What? What would it say? What word?

What senseless, inept phrase?

You said to me: that submerged city, that's our dark land.

There is nothing left of it but this waterway that traversed it. This river.

Have you forgotten?

Have you forgotten everything?

So cold, you said.

You said, that second city.

You said: stories languish all along this river, this riverine length, so gentle that you want to lie down next to it and move along with it.

Yes. You have forgotten everything.

Fog enters the garden.

It spreads over the river.

I see it.

It spreads over you. Over me.

The cat has stopped crying.
It is dead.

The cold and hunger.

And me, it's all the same to me.

I don't separate you from your body.

I don't separate you from me.

How to make it so that we lived that love?

How?

How to make it so that this love was lived?

It's strange…

It's through this skinny and wild cat, now dead, through this motionless garden all around it, that I reach you

Through this white whiteness, this infinite fog, that I reach your body.

My name is Aurélia Steiner.

I live in Melbourne where my parents are professors.

I am eighteen years old.

I write.

Aurélia Steiner
(Aurélia Vancouver)

I am in this room where I write to you each day. It's the middle of the day. The sky is dark. Before me is the sea. Today it is flat, heavy, seemingly as dense as iron and with no strength left to move. Between the sky and the water is a large black line, carbonized, thick. It covers the entire horizon, as even as a giant certain strikethrough, as significant as an insurmountable difference. It could be frightening.

In the mirror in my room, upright, veiled by the dark light, is my image. I look outside. The sailboats are stationary, sealed to the iron sea, still engaged in the movement where the vanished wind surprised them this morning.

I look at myself, I can't see myself clearly in the cold glass of the mirror. The light is so dark, it looks like night. I love you more than I can bear. I do not know you.

Now, between the horizon and the beach, something shifts in the depths of the sea. It is slow. It comes late, discovered though it was already there.

Against my body, this cold of the glass, this dead mirror. I no longer see anything of myself, I no longer see anything.

Now, now I begin to see again.

Before me a color is born, it is very intense, green, it occupies a part of the sea, it holds much of the sea in its color, a sea, but smaller, a sea within the whole of the sea. The light came from the bottom of the sea, from an excess of color in its depths, and this backlit black, a moment before, came from its sweeping eruption as it emerged from the sea. The sea becomes transparent, of the glimmer, of the brilliance of nocturnal organs, not like an emerald, you see, nor phosphorous, but like flesh.

I returned to my room very quickly to write you. I closed the doors and the windows. I am standing here with you as I discover the beach. I take a step back from the mirror. I look at myself. The eyes are blue, they say, the hair black. You see? blue, the eyes, beneath black hair. Oh how I love you, looking at me. I am so beautiful, to the point of becoming a stranger to myself. I smile at you and tell you my name.

My name is Aurélia Steiner. I am your child.

You are not aware of my existence.

You can give me no signal, death keeps you from seeing me, I know. And I, I see your death as a fleeting illusion of your life, the illusion, for example, of another love. It's all the same to me. I learn about you through myself. This morning, for example, through this momentary disappearance of the sea's movement, through this sudden horror for no apparent reason, I was aware of our deep resemblance faced with the accident of desire.

Sometimes others come. They are occasionally the age you would have been.

In a world where you are not alive, they take the place of our encounter. Through the adolescent grace and slenderness of the body I picture you in, through the clumsiness of your approach, the painful impatience, and sometimes, the tears, and also sometimes those cries for help on the brink of desire, there wouldn't be much of a difference between you and them if you, too, roamed the port's streets on your stopovers.

I give them my fresh body and they take it.

They speak to it. They say that they love it. They shout, they cry, they try and hurt me, I let them, I let them do it. Let them do it. Let them penetrate, shout their love, cry. You could have been one of them except for the fact that you would have seen me. You would have noticed this body, abandoned, offered, this pleasure swept far away from you and from which she refuses to return.

The sea, it seems. Its sound at the edge of the city.

Eyes closed, I would have asked you: what are you like? blond? a man from the North, with blue eyes? You would have been, but only slightly, slow to respond: blue eyes, yes, but my hair is black. Black? Yes.

I would have asked: are you looking for someone? someone they told you about? You say: that's right. You would continue: that's right, yes, someone I have no way of recognizing, whom I love more than I can bear.

I ask: Aurélia Steiner?

He does not answer. He moves away from me.

He shouts: how do you know?

I say that I have heard travelers speak of her on their stopovers. He asks. He cries.

I say: yes, all of them, were men with black hair.

In the closed room of the beach, alone, I construct your voice. You speak and I do not hear the story but only your voice. That of the ancient sleeper, your voice written henceforth, slimmed by time, freed from history. You would have left running and through the town I would have heard the cry of this name with no subject: Aurélia Steiner. I would have followed the echo of the sound of these two words until their disappearance. Then, gradually, I would have heard the mounting murmur of the sea. There would have been no wind.

I am still in this dark room facing the sea. I have been alone in this house for years. Everyone has left to find the calmer regions of the earth. Because of the storms, which are terrible here.

In the afternoon a slow separation took place between the black and green waters of the sea. The immense puddle blued. Movement returned to the surface. The sea shivered as if struck by a sudden wind. There was no wind. The night, which was coming.

I opened the doors and windows and a soft light entered my room.

The horizon was once more even, smooth, clear.

My mother died in childbirth on the plank beds of the camp. Burned alive with the others in the gas chambers. Aurélia Steiner my mother looks before her at the large white rectangle of the camp's roll call square. She suffers for a long time. At her side the child is alive.

The whole sea is now blue again. As always at this hour a great brightness emerges, just before a broad darkening cast by the night's reddish glow.

I cry without sadness. Night falls over absence, you see, always.

Here the vast orange and gold beaches of the sky over the sea.

Beneath the color, the sea shines, already faded.

Sometimes you think the final frontier of the day has been reached, but no.

Now the gold of the sky becomes milky. And then, gray.

There is nothing I can do about the eternity that I carry to the place of your final gaze, upon the white rectangle of the camp's roll call square.

It was the summer. Death was overcoming you.

You could still see I think, but already you no longer suffered, already in a state of numbness.

You were bathing in the blood of my birth. I was lying at your side in the dust of the earth.

All around you, firm and cracked with sun, that foreign land, that light, that perfect summer, that warm sky.

Before you, the white rectangle in which he dies.

The storm arrived in the night. A little after midnight, with the start of the second day, the wind.

Here it is.

And then her, the sea. She yielded to this wind, followed along.

It began with a bestial clamor. The violence was such that in the memory of mankind there had never been anything so terrible.

The sea assaulted the city, she climbed over, invaded.

She broke glass, smashed doors and windows, burst through walls, carried off roofs and the city remained thus, opened, gaping to the wind. In the sudden lull that occurred, as she regained her strength and her breath, you could hear people chanting their final prayers at the top of their lungs.

With the lightning, you could see them, standing in their gutted homes.
I listened to the cries of the sea.

When we thought we had reached the other side of the storm, just before dawn, in the livid lightness of daybreak, the great salt reservoirs exploded beneath the long white swells of the North Pacific. The salt spread through the sea. Her salinity became fatal. She passed from life to death in a matter of seconds.

The day broke.
And so, heavy, poisoned, the sea became calm.

In the white rectangle of the roll call square my mother Aurélia Steiner can still see the hanged soup thief squirming at the end of his rope, too thin, too light, he cannot hang himself with his own weight. It is the morning of the second day.

My mother, eighteen, dies. Before her, at the end of his rope, he calls to her, shouts his mad love. She can no longer hear him.

Here is the place in the world where you can find Aurélia Steiner. She can be found here and nowhere else in the lands of societies protected against her, the sea.

She hears the entire world struggle against the same fear, she sees that what is happening here spreads throughout the world.

She sees that the center of this fear is now shifting. That it revolves around her.
She sees that the entire world is afraid of her, her, Aurélia Steiner.

The next morning the city is still soaked, the sea withdraws from the invaded lands, the streets, the gardens, the cathedrals. The port ships are lying on their sides, demasted. The beaches are covered in dead fish, suffocated by the salt of the reservoirs. The religious have left the city's outskirts, they have come to collect the dead fish to feed the orphans of the world, they are singing hymns of gratitude.

In the frozen sky the sun is harsh and full. The whole city sleeps in this stark and immaculate daylight of a stormy sky. I go into town, drowsy beneath this frightening sun. The sea is there, in her place, holed up. Twitching, she shouts once more then falls back asleep, a child's sleep streaked with nightmares. The city is white with salt, petrified in the chaos the sea has left it in.

I walk.

Little by little, without my sensing it, you return to me from the exile of the night, the underside of the world, that dark shadow where you stand. You cross the city. I see you reach a hotel by the port. Today you are a sailor with black hair. Tall. Still the skin and bones of youth or hunger. You turned around, you hesitated and then you wandered off. I know that when night falls you will come to this street and look for her, her, the one you passed in town this morning, whom you watched. Perhaps because of that airy dress and that blue gaze beneath black hair.

I went to lie down on the depths of the sea, facing the frozen sky. She was still feverish, warm.

Little girl. Love. Little child.

I called her by many names, by the name of Aurélia, Aurélia Steiner.

In her depths she still struggled between depletion and the desire to kill.

At times, vast movements roused her, the flanks of an animal turning round in circles before taking back their place in the litter.

Love, love, all those things that speak for us. You, child, the sea.

I told her the state of the city.

Then, I told her the story.

She was under my back, ten meters thick? eight-hundred meters?

The difference was nonexistent.

Her surface was purely illusory, flesh without skin, an open gash, a silk of icy air.

I spoke to her for a long time. I told her the story. I spoke to her of those lovers in the white rectangle of death. I sang. I was speaking, singing, and I could hear the story. I felt her beneath me, mineral, with the irrefutable strength of God.

When I returned, a newsboy was shouting a headline about the anger of the sea. He described the extent of the damage and said there had been no human victims.

People came out to buy the paper.

I went back to my room, I rinsed my body and hair with fresh-water and waited for the young sailor with black hair. As I wait for him, I write you.

As I tremble with desire for him, I love you.

I gather them through you and from their number I make you. You are what will never take place and what, thus, is lived. From all of them you always emerge unique, inexhaustible place of the world, unquenchable love.

You are finally dead, they have taken you down, you are lying down, doubled over in a pose of abandon, of sleep, of a child.

The white rectangle of the roll call square is empty except for your body.

The lovers are dead.

You had stolen soup for the little girl, Aurélia. They caught you. They hanged you.

Above you, for three days in a row, the German sky, before your eyes that sky full of water and fertile rains.

For three days in a row you had called from the end of your rope, you had shouted, repeated endlessly that a child named Aurélia Steiner had just been born in the camp, you had asked that she be fed, that she not be given to the dogs. You had howled, pleaded with the world, that the little Aurélia Steiner not be forgotten.

Around the evening of the third day, a bullet was shot through your skull, to put an end to the disturbance.

She, she was dead upon morning. At her side, the child was alive.

The words Aurélia Steiner no longer rang through the camp. They were taken up elsewhere, on other decks, in other parts of the world.

Around evening, here, there are still bursts of light at the horizon, even though it was overcast the entire day, even though it rained, the clouds, for an instant, part and let through the light of the sun.

Evening, again.

I saw him as light struck the sleeping sea.

I closed my eyes.

I've just done it. Apparently I stopped writing you.

And so, sometimes, I see the liquid and blue color of the empty eyes, already taken by death, of the young man hanged in the roll call square. I see his youth also.

Eighteen, also. And yet he had reached his full size.

I do not know his name.

I do not see the mother on the plank bed. Nothing of her, except the gesture of hiding the child.

The sailor with black hair is behind the open window. He watches me.

He asks where I'm from. I say I don't know.

He says he was on the beach while I was bathing in the sea.

He can't quite remember who he met in town this morning, he must have met someone else. I ask which one he desires. He says the one from this morning.

I tell him that was me.

I tell him: I will give you a name.

You are going to pronounce it, you will not understand why and yet I'm asking you to do it, to repeat it without under-

standing, as if there were something to understand.

I say the name. Aurélia Steiner.

I write it on a blank page and I give it to him.

He slowly deciphers it and looks at me to see if he has read it correctly.

I say nothing. I lie down next to him.

He repeats the name, he sees that I am listening.

He is clumsy at first, not sure which language to say it in, then he throws the paper away, he comes to me and looks at me and speaks to me with the name.

He takes my dress off carefully. He has, it seems, plenty of time at his disposal.

He begins to discover the body of Aurélia Steiner.

She still does not look, her eyes closed on the white rectangle of death.

Sometimes he says the full name.

Sometimes he says just the first name.

Sometimes just the last name.

He no longer knows how to say any other word.

He says them in kisses, lips against skin, he says them softly, he shouts them, he calls them inside the body, against the mouth, against the wall. He battles them. Sometimes he stays still with a restraint that makes him moan, then he seems to forget the names, and then very softly, he speaks them again with painful effort as if their very pronunciation was the cause of this pain.

He says: Juden, Juden Aurélia, Juden Aurélia Steiner.

He holds himself at the entrance of the body of Aurélia Steiner, remains there, still extremely careful to see the torture through to its end. Then he enters the body.

In a very slow movement, inverse to his impulse, he enters the body of Aurélia Steiner.

The slowness makes the lovers scream.

Once more, he speaks the names, he repeats them so softly, again.

He spoke the names again, he repeated them again, but without a voice, in an oblivious brutality, in an unfamiliar accent.

I woke up at dawn.

The sailor with black hair was lying on the floor of my room. He was watching me.

I fell back asleep. I heard him say that his eyes were burning from having seen the beauty of Aurélia Steiner. That his boat was leaving at noon but he would not be on board, that the boat would leave without him, that he wanted to stay with her, Aurélia Steiner, no matter the consequences.

I told him that I did not belong to anyone in particular. That I was not my own person.

My name is Aurélia Steiner.

I live in Vancouver, where my parents are professors.

I am eighteen years old.

I write.

Aurélia Steiner
(Aurélia Paris)

Today, beyond the windows is the forest and the wind has arrived. The roses were over there in that other country in the North. The little girl doesn't know them. She never saw the roses, now dead, nor the fields nor the sea.

The little girl is at the tower window and she looks out at the forest, she has slightly opened the black curtains and she looks out at the ocean of the forest. The rain has stopped. It's nearly night but under the window, above the trees, the sky is still blue. The tower is square, very tall, made from black cement. The little girl is on the top floor, she sees other towers further on, also black. She has never gone down into the forest.

The little girl leaves the window and starts to sing a foreign song in a language she doesn't understand. She has not yet completely closed the window curtain and we still see light in the bedroom. She looks at herself in the mirror. She sees black hair and the brightness of the eyes. The eyes are a very dark blue, they lose their color with the night and then they are nothing but limpid bottomless darkness. The little girl is unaware. She says she has always known the song. Doesn't remember having learned it.

Someone is crying. It's the woman who watches over the little girl, who bathes her and feeds her. The apartment is large, almost empty, almost everything was sold. The woman stands in the entryway, seated on a chair, next to her is a revolver. The little girl has always seen her there, waiting for the German police so she can kill. Night and day, the little girl doesn't know for how many years, the woman waits. What the little girl knows is that as soon as she hears the word polizeï behind the door the woman will open it and kill everyone, first the police and then afterwards the two of them.

The little girl goes to close the black double curtains then she goes to her bed and lights the little iron lantern. Under the lamp, the cat. It stands under the light. Around it, pell-mell, are newspapers detailing the most recent Reich army operations with which the woman taught the little girl how to write. Next to the cat, still and stiff, is a dead butterfly the color of dust, it has a large hairy head like a dog, its eyes are bulging, still wide open onto death. The fear must have been terrible before killing.

The little girl sits down on the bed opposite the cat. The cat yawns stretches and sits opposite her. Their eyes are at the same height. They stare at each other. The purring of the cat suddenly grows as it stares at the child, it grows even more, it fills the universe. A hurricane is trapped inside the cat, very muted, very far within the cat but sometimes nearly extricates itself from the cat, rasping, a moan of wild happiness. Now, the Jewish song, the little girl sings it for the cat. The cat lies down on the table and the little girl pets it, her hand runs over the cat's body and suddenly she presses down hard on the flattened crushed form of the living cat—it can't breathe, it's scared—the cat struggles, tries to flee—then the little girl loosens her grip and speaks to the cat with loving words. The purring of the cat resumes, the little girl puts her ear against the warm stomach and fills herself with it. Then she takes the dead butterfly, she shows it to the cat, watches it with a grimace, for a laugh, and then drops it and sings the Jewish song again. Then the eyes of the cat and of the little girl stare at each other until they can't see anymore.

From the depths of the sky suddenly, there it is. The war. The sound. From the hallway the woman shouts to close the curtains, not to forget. The hunks of steel begin to pass over the forest.

"Speak to me," cries the woman.

"Another six minutes," says the little girl. "Close your eyes."

The roof of approaching noise, the death charge, the bellies full of bombs, smooth, ready to open. The little girl says:

"They're here. Close your eyes."

The little girl looks at her little skinny hands on the cat. They tremble like the walls, the windows, the air, the towers in their entirety, the mass of forest.

"Come," cries the woman.

It's still happening. They are there a little longer than the little girl said. The bellies with the fine blue steel skin, full, full of children. And then at the most intense moment, brutally, the other sound. That of the sharp shells of the anti-aircraft guns. The little girl listens, waits, listens again to the wind through the steel and then speaks to the cat.

"It's near the Rhine. Cologne."

Nothing has fallen from the sky, no drop, no clamor. The little girl listened closely, nothing.

"Where are they going?" cries the woman.

"Berlin," says the child.

The woman cries.

"Come."

The little girl leaves the cat and goes to see the woman, crosses the dark apartment. There she is. There it's light. There, no window, no opening to the outside, it's the end of the hallway that leads to the entry door, where they must enter. A lightbulb hanging from the wall illuminates the war. The woman is there surveilling the life of a child. She has left her knitting on her knees. We hear nothing except, in the distance, the anti-aircraft guns firing off one after another. The little one sits at the woman's feet and says to her:
"The cat killed a butterfly."

The woman and the little girl remain intertwined for a long time, crying and quieting cheerfully as they do every night.

"I cried again," says the woman, "every day I cry over the admirable mistake of life."

They laugh. The woman caresses her hair, the tangle of silk, the shiny black curls. The sound grows farther from the forest. The woman leans over and smells the child's hair, eats it, she says that in her mouth this hair smells like the sea.

"Listen, they're passing over the Rhine," says the child.

"Yes."

There is no more sound except for the gusts of wind that pass blindly and disturb and destroy the stillness of the forest.

"Where are they going?" asks the woman.

"Berlin," says the child.

"That's right," says the woman, "that's right…"

They laugh. The woman asks:

"What will become of us?"

"We will die," says the child, "you will kill us."

"Yes," says the woman—she stops laughing—"you're cold"—she touches her arm.

The little girl doesn't answer the woman.

"The cat, I call it Aranahancha."—the child laughs.

"Aranahancha," repeats the woman.

The little girl laughs very hard. The woman laughs with her and then she closes her eyes and touches the little girl's body and moans.

"You're skinny," says the woman, "your little bones beneath the skin."

The little girl laughs at everything the woman says.

And then they start to sing the Jewish song. Then the woman lets the child sing alone, and for the hundredth time tells her the story.

"Apart from this little rectangle of white cotton sown inside your dress," says the woman, "that first day, we knew nothing, you and I. On the white rectangle there were the letters A. S. and a birthdate. You are seven years old."

The little girl listens to the silence. She says:

"Yes, it must be Berlin."

She stands up and violently pushes the woman away, nearly strikes her, then she shouts wordlessly then she stands up and returns to her bedroom. Crosses the dark hallways. Skinny, so thin, disturbs nothing, knocks against nothing. She must be back in the bedroom. The woman hears her singing.

In the dark bedroom, the cat is still sitting up. In the lampshade, a crackling. There's a fly. The cat listens. It's not purring anymore. The crackling has stopped. The cat forgets the fly. Once again, it looks at the child. The child listens to the porous immensity of the night. She says:

"Yes, it's Berlin."

The crackling resumes. The cat sits up, turns towards the lampshade and with its paw pats it with a restrained and nervous gesture. It figured out that the sound came from there. It listens as the child listens through the thickness of the night.

Beneath the lamp the eyes of the cat shine with a mineral perfection, the child sees them obliquely as she listens, their color is first a colorless transparency, then there is a green ring striped with tiny channels where gold flows, that ring gleams, it surrounds a black hole through which the cat sees.

Now, they return. The anti-aircraft guns once more against the smooth bellies of blue steel. They strike, try to rip open, puncture.

"Listen," says the child.

The sound increases, methodical, long, a river, a continuous surge, the full sound. Less heavy than on the way there.

"None were hit," says the child. "They all came back."

An old fly from the summer comes out of the lampshade, wavering. From zone to zone, the sirens, the guns strike against the blue emptied bellies. They grow distant. The fly doesn't have the strength to take flight anymore. However it manages to leave the top of the table; it moves further into the bedroom. The cat has lost sight of it. The planes grow distant and their distancing renders more perceptible the sounds of the fly's agony.

"Fifty thousand dead," says the child.

The cat has stopped purring. The child has completely lost interest in it. A rather long time passes. The sound subsides. The cat's eyes are fixed, they stare at the end of the bedroom. It knows that's where the fly disappeared, the sound. The planes, even farther towards the ocean. The child starts to sing again. The fly, once more, tries to take flight. Exhausted buzzing. It tries. It lands everywhere, out of strength each time, with shorter and shorter intervals. The cat, sure of the outcome, waits. Its aggravation increases, it contains it.

"They're passing over the sea," says the child, "listen."

Isolated, useless, another few anti-aircraft gun strikes. The fly takes off for a second and falls flat, crumbles against a wall. It makes a sound that is recognizable to the child and to the cat, that of a massacre. For a few seconds there's no more sound. From time to time only the reflections of the woman in the entryway on the future of children. The cat listens—to the fly—for another short moment. Then, since the fly doesn't come back, it forgets about it. It looks again at the child. Then there is the purring of the cat in the night which has become so calm. The woman says that the children will all be killed. The child laughs. She points out the woman to the cat. She says:

"She's crying again."

The cat stretches and gives a big yawn. Its gray fur splits and the interior of its mouth appears, white of the teeth, pink in between.

"Listen to that," now she's afraid.

The cat digs its claws into the blotting paper on the desk and, in a gesture of restraint, withdraws them. It's still hungry for the fly.
"I am Jewish," says the child.

The fly emerges one last time from its coma. Its buzzing resumes, more hollow, noisy, as if drunk. This is the end. The elytra are out of strength, they can't circulate enough air to hold up the body. The fly now lives a chaotic, broken existence.

"Jewish," says the child.

The fly falls like a meteorite onto the blotting paper on the desk between the child and the cat. The cat sits up. The fly contorts in a difficult death. It can't fly anymore. The cat lifts its paw. Places it on the fly. The child watches without seeing. The fly makes a crackling sound under the cat's paw. The paw remains soft for a moment, gentle, joyous, the cat doesn't press down.

"I remember my mother," says the child.

The cat withdraws its paw from on top of the fly. A detached wing is on the desk. The other wing is still on the fly, it still beats and drags the body around and around in a dead-end. The fly tries again to take flight. It can't anymore.

"My mother, she was the queen of the Jews," says the child. "Queen of Jerusalem and Samaria. Then the whites came, they took her away."

She gestures at the woman in the entryway.

"She doesn't know."

The cat watches the diabolical circling of the fly's mutilated body. The child listens again to the thickness of the air over the forest. The cat makes up its mind, leans its head and delicately, without greed, takes the fly in its mouth, makes large chewing motions, excessive, ridiculous—the fly is so small that the cat can't feel it in its teeth—and all at once, swallows it.

The cat licks its paw and sits back down opposite the child. She moves her hand towards the cat, the cat charges at this hand, rubs its whole body against it in a relentless gesture of love. The child leaves her hand open to the approaches of the cat's body.

"Sometimes I want to die," says the child—she adds—"My father, I don't know who he was, probably a traveler, he came from Syria."

The cat's delirium now knows no bounds. It lunges at the child with its head lowered in an almost violent motion, under the influence of the child's gentle voice saying it wants to die the cat rubs its side against her chest. She, she is listening to what's happening outside, the war, the forest. She says:

"Here they are again."

In the distance, the beginning of a rumble, slight but unfailing. The child takes the cat and places it on the ground. She says:

"Go away."

In the entryway the woman hears the second death charge, the long convoy of materials, the bombs.

"Where is it this time?" asks the woman.

"Düsseldorf," says the child.

"That's right," says the woman.

With a leap the cat returns to the desk, still trembling with desire.

"Go away," says the child.

She has placed her head on the desk, she has no more face. In the distance, the woman in the hallway lists the cities of the Palatinate and asks God to massacre the evil, the German peoples. She recites a prayer the child doesn't know. The cat, with all its strength, tries to work its way under the child's face, to slide itself between her hair and her forehead. The muffled voice under the hair:

"Go away, go away."

No, the cat does not want to go away.

The child takes the cat and places it on the ground.

The cat stops insisting. It rubs itself against the desk legs and then leaves. It has left the room, it's in the dark hallways near the woman. The child hears the slight creak of the floor beneath its paws. Now it's farther away. She hears everything. Then there is nothing left, except, in the distance, the mass of death, thick and continuous, which approaches the tower.

"Are there a lot of them?" asks the woman from the end of the hallway.

"A hundred," says the child.

Now they're above the forest. As if they were about to attack the tower. The child turns off the desk lamp. She lies down with her head in her hands. She shouts to the woman.

"I hope they fall."

The woman can't hear very well. She says that someone shouted and that she's afraid, in the middle of the night who could that be? The child shouts:

"I want to die."

The racket is so intense that her head is filled with it, the walls, the forest, no one is breathing anymore, everyone closes their eyes, goes quiet, except for the child who shouts, who calls for death. She cries into her hands. The anti-aircraft guns have begun to shoot at the full bellies again. The planes have slowed down it seems. It seems that a belly full of children has just burst. The child shouts.

"Maman," shouts the child.

The woman heard it too. She shouts, she asks what it is, what is it? The child says that the tower has been hit and that they're going to die. And then she laughs.

The woman has not understood. She starts again to list the cities on the Rhine and to ask God to exterminate the evil, the world. She doesn't pray anymore, she recites German geography lessons she learned as a child. Everything she says is punctured by the whistling of the anti-aircraft guns. The lantern has gone out. The child goes quiet. The woman calls her, she is in the dark, she is afraid. And then, suddenly that noise, that enormous screech of the fall, and then nothing more. The child shouts:

"The forest."

The sound of the squadron diminishes, the cannons follow the contingent, go farther and farther. The war grows distant. The light doesn't return. The fallen plane is left alone. The child goes to the window and lifts the black curtains. There is an enormous fire at the bottom of the tower, solitary. The struck plane. It illuminates the entire forest. The black sky.

"Come," yells the woman.

The child goes.

"It's over," says the woman. "Are you here?"

Yes. She says that the forest is ablaze, right there, beneath the tower. That everything is deserted apart from the fire. That to-

morrow where the plane is, there will be a black hole in the forest. She takes a candle along the wall—she sees the child in the dark—and she lights it. And she sings the Jewish song. She is sitting on the ground at the woman's feet. And she sings the Jewish song and the woman begins gently to fall asleep to Aurélia Steiner's song.

"They'll come back from where?" asks the woman.

"Liège," says Aurélia.

"That's right, that's right," says the woman.

Aurélia resumes the Jewish song. The woman falls asleep and starts to speak.

"If I had known," says the woman, "well, let's not talk about it anymore, especially since I have nothing against that little girl... nothing... I would have preferred for other Jews to take care of her, and younger people... but how? The two of them left in the night, a train of thirteen trucks, but left for where? and how to prove that she is their child? how?... if they return, say they do, why not?... she is growing up too quickly, the little girl, they say it's the lack of food... seven years after the little white rectangle on her jumper..."

Aurélia has stopped singing. She listens to the woman who holds her story. Sometimes she bursts out laughing and the woman wakes up. She asks what's wrong, who spoke and where they are.

"Nijmegen," says Aurélia. "They're passing over."

The woman says that she loves this little girl, very much, that she doesn't know why. Then she goes quiet. Then she says again that she loves her and how much. Then she goes quiet again. Then Aurélia shakes her gently.

"Tell me," says Aurélia.—She waits, the woman is sleeping, so Aurélia dictates for her—"so she took off running, she brought me?"

"That's right," says the sleeping woman.

Aurélia waits. Then she asks: "Who?"

"Your mother," says the woman.

"'Take the little one, I have something urgent to do'"? asks Aurélia.

"That's right," says the woman, "'I have something urgent to do, I'll be back in ten minutes.'"

"Noise in the stairwell?'"

"Yes," says the woman. "The German police."

"Then nothing?" asks Aurélia.

"Then nothing," says the woman.

"Never, never?"

"Never."

Aurélia goes quiet. The woman sings the Jewish song that Aurélia sings. Aurélia puts her head on the woman's knees. She says:

"Where is the cat?"

The woman caresses Aurélia's black hair. Then her hand stops. She doesn't answer. She asks a final time:

"So? Where are they?"

"Liège," says Aurélia, "they're going back."

"So?" asks the woman, "the one who's dead?"

"Nothing," says Aurélia.

Aurélia squeezes the woman in her arms. The woman moans.

"Kiss me kiss me," says Aurélia.

The woman makes an effort and caresses Aurélia's hair, then she loses strength, sleep takes over. From zone to zone in the city the sirens sound the all clear.

"Tell me her name," shouts Aurélia.

"Steiner," says the woman. "Steiner Aurélia. That's what the police were shouting."

The cat. It returns from an adjoining room. It's still half-asleep, it yawns. It sees Aurélia, goes to her, lies down against her.

"They're passing over the sea," says Aurélia.

Aurélia starts to pet the cat, first distractedly then harder and harder. The cat watches for Aurélia's hand and bites it, but without doing any harm. Aurélia calls the woman.

"He ate a fly, too," shouts Aurélia.

The woman is asleep. She doesn't answer.

Already, at the windows, day. It enters the hallway of war.

The cat lies on its back, it purrs with wild desire for Aurélia. Its tawny belly spreads like a loess. Aurélia lies next to the cat. The cat licks Aurélia's forehead. Its purring fills Aurélia's head. She is as if dead, Aurélia, and the cat plays with her as it did a moment ago with the fly, one of the first of the summer.

"My mother," says Aurélia, "she was named Aurélia Steiner."

Aurélia places her head against the cat's stomach. The stomach is warm, it contains the purring of the cat which is bigger than the cat, a buried continent.

"Steiner Aurélia," says Aurélia. "Like me."

Still in that bedroom where I write to you. Today, beyond the windows, was the forest and the wind had arrived.

The roses are dead in that other country in the North, rose by rose, carried off by the winter.

I cried again. Sometimes I think I can see your hand through my hand, the one that never touched me. I see it pass over my body, so free so alone, wild with knowledge and separated from your desire, from you, from me. It moves. Touches. And knows things about me, the kind of things that I do not know.

It's night. Now I can no longer see the words written down. I can no longer see anything but my motionless hand that has stopped writing you. But beneath the window pane the sky is still blue. The blue of Aurélia's eyes would have been darker, you see, especially at night, then it would have lost its color to become limpid bottomless darkness.

My name is Aurélia Steiner.

I live in Paris where my parents are professors.

I am eighteen years old.

I write.

Olivia Baes is a French-American writer, translator, and filmmaker. Her work explores how inner states shape perception, with a focus on dismantling the male gaze. She co-translated *The Easy Life* and *Me & Other Writing* by Marguerite Duras along with *Into the Sun* by C.-F. Ramuz (New Directions). Her debut feature, *Je suis fleur*—a Franco-Spanish co-pro-duction between Buffalo Films and Imagic—is currently in post-production, developed from a short screenplay that won the 2021 Lights On contest. She is the curator of the James Baes Foundation and, in 2025, co-curated two exhibitions of her father's work with Eva Pritsky Gallery, in Paris and at the Basel Social Club. Her work has appeared in The New Yorker, The Paris Review, and The End.

Emma Ramadan is a literary translator of over forty books from French, including co-translations with Olivia Baes of Marguerite Duras's *Me & Other Writing* and *The Easy Life*, and Charles Ferdinand Ramuz's *Into the Sun*. She is the recipient of two NEA Fellowships, the PEN Translation Prize, the Albertine Prize, and the James Tait Black Prize, among others.

Published by Inpatient Press / Mercurial Editions
First edition: New York City, September 2025

Distributed by The MIT Press